Our Locust Years

Poems by Corey Mesler

UNBOUND
CONTENT

Englewood, NJ

ISBN 978-1-936373-41-3
Published in the United States by Unbound Content, LLC,
Englewood, NJ.
Cover art: Hilltop ©2012 by Rebecca Tickle
Author photo: ©2012, by Irma Idell

Our Locust Years
First edition 2013

UNBOUND
CONTENT

For my mother, Sadie Mesler

Table of Contents

As nights went on and nothing happened and the phenomenon slowly faded to the accustomed deeper violets again, most had difficulty remembering the earlier rise of heart, the sense of overture and possibility, and went back once again to seeking only orgasm, hallucination, stupor, sleep, to fetch them through the night and prepare them against the day.

—Thomas Pynchon

The night does funny things inside a man.

—Tom Waits

Witch Philosophy

Naïve people know nothing of the One Inside Who Doesn't Wish You Well,
and think that their enemies are all in the outside world.

—Robert Bly

She said, all spells have curative
powers but all spells
have side effects, too, like
preternatural pills.
She said, find a still place.
Spells work in stillness.
Stillness is a spell.
And the sickness you want cured
perhaps should not be cured.
Suffering can be alleviated, she said.
But sickness is sometimes
binding, requisite; sickness is sometimes
a spell itself. The gods
are not doctors. She said, concentrate
your mind. Let the spell
be the thing your heart reads, the
stillness, the instructive infection.

Writ(ing)

The teacher said anything can start
a poem.
Like this: I woke up to find
the coffee tin empty.

The teacher said anything can start
your head.
Like this: the way in is equal to the
way out.

Anticipation Is a Blind Dog in a Meat Shop

I wait at the curb
for the new novel to arrive.
In the gutter runs a stream
past Eve and Adam's.
A small boat appears.
On it a family heading for
a new life, risking everything.
They distract me momentarily.
Then, in the wavy distance,
I see a truck. On it
perhaps the new novel.
I pick up a stick. I may sink
the little boat, sink
the family's plans. Every-
thing depends on
my getting, soon, the new novel.

A White Pause

The shaft
of sunlight,
which lay across
your sleeping face,
looked cool
as if a white washcloth
had been placed there
to calm a fever.
I almost had to cross
the room and
rest my hand in it.

Chloe Blooming

While my daughter sleeps
her head is filling with fervor.
She walks into the day,
fearless as the wind at sea.
Her enthusiasm for most things
shames my simple gloom.
Her voice can honey my antipathy.
Her voice can call me back,
crawling like a man who believes
he can still walk erect, that kind of ape.
I follow her, torn between parenting
and learning, between ape and god.

Corey Mesler

Church

When Bells stop ringing—Church—begins—
—Emily Dickinson

It was a chapel
built around a labyrinth.
In its rafters,
so far away as to be limitless,
were cranes of paper,
wings of man.
It was a chapel
where inclusion was sincere,
like a bible
that falls to different pages
each day. It was
a chapel shaped like a farm,
a place where
life blossomed, multivariate
and precise,
open-ended and delirious
as the tumult of dream.

Book

What book is this
splayed like
a Christ crucified
waiting for my
hand to come
and pluck it from
underneath the lamp's
calm umbrella?
It is a book of poems.
And in it I find this
line: I talk to God.
It is just a book
about talking to God.

Departure

Eight years ago
my father left

turning out the light
behind him,

leaving me to bake
a pie
with the scarecrow's bones.

The Earth Knows My Secret Love

I sleep beneath the rainbow
and wake from dreams
of your humid core.
The sky knows my infidelity.
The earth, brown and
worm-etched, knows my secret
love. It is the Sabbath
here in my perimeter. This
means I pray. I pray for
more dreams, for fidelity, and
for a return to your core,
full of pure, unbroken sky.

And Her Name Was I Am Not Staying

She entered my life
like a battered dresser, all
drawers open, a
pyknic smudged with dark
that beckoned.
I opened up the last pair
of pants I owned.
She said, I won't take this
lying down, just so
you know. I said, I don't care,
I only came here for the
retribution. I said, I
wanted you at first, as
a balance, some kind of
statement. She said, stop
the palaver, cowpoke,
and brand me till
I say to stop. She was that
kind of wayward.
She was crazy as a star.
She spoke in fluent hurt.
And now, when I think of
her, and I do, a lot,
I remember her phony
medals, her thighs carved from
adamant, and the way she
made me a better man,
by kicking the dust out
of me, by making me survive
her unexpected absence,
like a cored apple, like
hope upon a rocking deathbed.

More About Wendy Ward

She was dark brown
like a horse's shadow,
and so lovely my heart
hurt. I approached her
with a courage that now
I cannot fathom. This
was many years ago
in the kingdom of youth.
She is even now beautiful.
Sometimes, now, she
will answer if I call. But
mostly she is still distant,
a smudge of memory,
something that tugs at you
but is, in a real sense,
invisible, irretrievable, mute.

Corey Mesler

In This Atmosphere

I want to read your book.
I want you to read mine.
It is in this atmosphere
that we must survive.
The things the television tells
me are not the things
that I want to talk about.
I have higher aspirations.
I will say, I love your similes.
You will smile and answer,
Your talk makes me listen.
I wish the world could be
like this. I wish we could
reach each other so easily.
I hold out my jacket. The
blurbs on it are a lie. You
hold out your spine.
It is in this atmosphere
that we may survive.
It is in this atmosphere
that love blooms, all along
the margins, all along the
fore-edge, all for us, the
adventurers, the easy riders.

I Didn't Know It Was Going to Be
a Frank O'Hara Day

I didn't know it was going to be
a Frank O'Hara day
until I walked outside and suddenly
it was New York
and the sidewalk was painted by
Jasper Johns and
the women all were beautiful in
their dying cigarette youth.
I didn't know it was going to be
a Frank O'Hara day
until I found myself in a bar sur-
rounded by poets,
all asking me to go naked into the
screaming rhinestone fandango night.

Iconolatry

You placed your ankles
on my shoulders
as I entered you.
It was quite a trick.
You were an athlete, a killer
softball shortstop.
Your legs were strong as
the mainstay of the
laboring bark.
I was younger then, still
entirely flummoxed by your
incandescent beauty.
You left me, of course, and
before you did you
undermined my confidence
with your diffident, dying
love. That's the
way the story is written. That's
its power, as story, as dream.
Still, I have that image,
your legs so open I thought I
would be welcome forever, forever.

My Heart a Map

It was a map,
looked like a poem.
It was just a face,
a frozen past.
I held it in my mind
for one second
too long.
My heart began to
spill, over and
over, a generator.
My heart of silk,
a lake's reflective surface.
My heart a map.

Again Lita

She was my first kiss.
It was in a game
at an 8th grade party.
On my death bed
I plan on asking her
to bring me full circle.
In between I have
had many lovers, two
wives, two children.
My life has been complete.
At times I think it
has been complete.
I wrote a book of poems
about her, about the
one intimate moment we
shared in front of the
entire 8th grade class.
She answered my phone
call with the voice
that over the years
has come to seem like
paradise to me. "Hello,
sap," she said. I wrote
it down. That's why it,
like you, is part of this.

Out Near the Chemical Plant

Out near the chemical plant,
where my father worked his whole life,
there are fields of corn, glistening,
green and yellow, full of life.
The sun catches stalks and they dance.
There is also a black fungus called ergot.
It is poisonous and hallucinogenic.
No one is blaming the chemical plant.
Now my father is gone and
the plant lives on, pumping out its
heady interfusions, creating God knows what,
in secret, after dark, with towers
of flame high above the Schlenk flasks,
and acid baths, and burettes, and alembics,
and men in white coats and badges,
who pledge their nights to experiment,
to the Company, to the very human belief
that there is better living through chemistry.

Corey Mesler

Our Locust Years

Meg opened me like a cardboard box.
She shook me and bugs fell out.
I limned around for a year and half.
The meanings I had gleaned from other
substances shone like cataracts.
My eyes crusted over like a pie.
Meg returned to me years later.
She carried a third leg, a hollow laugh.
We began living together like kittens.
Some days we don't wake up till
the neighbors stop shooting.
Some days we don't wake up at all.
It's just the way things happen here.
It's just the tricky way we were taut.
Here in the columbarium, our locust years.

Over, Easy

The sun is a yolk.
The sky is teeming
with oxen.
I can't breathe, I say to
my co-pilot.
I made you that way, he
snaps back.
It's tougher at night.
The prayer
is rusted.
Then logic goes,
leaving you stranded like a de-
throned god. Stranded
and loving it like hell.

The Best Effects Available

The face in the coffeepot
is unfamiliar. The dog
whines and dines
on the back stoop. My wife
stoops to add a bit
of catfood to his diet. The
seventh son arrives
just in time for the timer
to go off. It goes off
early. At dinner we are all
gathered at the stable.
The face I carried from the
breakfast eggs to this
is one long whisper.
It says, we age, we change,
the best we can do is
hold up our and. And, that's
the final thought as
the sunset shoots through
the bedroom walls
in what we take as the
best effects currently available.

Pinprick

Little poem about the memory of your sweet skin and the way it felt so young and full of life like the apple's peel in the garden before the fall.

Shift

Next to a gravestone/a green tin cup
brimful of shadows./Must we drink?
—Jim Harrison and Ted Kooser
from *Braided Creek*

We used to talk of death as if
it were Tahiti
or the Balkans. It was that remote.
Now, the mirror
is unkind and the women, in their
skirts, don't even turn around.

It Was Summer, of That I Am Sure

In the mild summer heat
what we stripped down to
was our best selves.
Your lap was full of pomegranates.
My eyes wouldn't focus.
And, on the tennis courts, you ran
like a young colt. I
watched you like a man condemned
to stand outside
where it is always summer, but
where a man loses himself over and
over, his heart a sore.

Writing Myself

I wrote a letter to myself.
I mailed it years
ago from the city where
you and I coincided.
I still await it, here in the
new place, where the
walls are so white you'd swear
you've gone blind.
Outside I hear the mooing of
doves. The sun sets
like a table of china. And I speak
your name softly
to the dust on the encyclopedia.

I Didn't Know I Was Going to Do That

The house rocks like a cradle.
It is light like a candle, like moss.
I am lulled toward sleep
as a boat is pulled from shore
toward the imaginary horizon.
I lie down to avoid falling. The
phone whispers in the corner where
it sits, a defiance. I open a
new mouth and the same song comes
out. I say your name until
it disappears. Now I can start again.
I read the phone book the way I once
read The Dream Songs. I misspell the
incantation. I say to the drapes, thank
you for the dim. I say to my shadow,
I didn't know I was going to do that.

Corey Mesler

He Sit Ate

The afternoon we let the horses
loose you turned to me
like a question. I put my lap under
your lap. The way
the room tilted this way and that
made us ask things
of each other. The quiet in my head
was you disappearing.
I longed to be long in the answering.

We At Her

A change in the weather
Is known to be extreme.

—Bob Dylan

Just yesterday in this spot
it was hot as glass.
Today the prevailing winds
bring in the experimental
poets and their adverbial anger.
Our team is playing
tonight so the city is quiet,
like that moment right before
the preacher coughs.
I take Marsha's hand. She
blinks back a rip
in the space/time continuum.
Later we will buy a house
and try to call it Spot.
For now, we have our fingers
in the wind. Something
is speaking to us, something from
far away, in another novel.

Corey Mesler

Writing Like Myself

I write like myself.
This is both good and bad.
At least, I say to you,
I am past that thorny patch
where I wrote like you.
You were never comfortable
with me. You were always
the one to hang up first.
Now, as I write this, I see
your face, suspended, white
and severe over the page
like a statute meant to topple.
I couldn't be happier today,
the words like tiny sores.

Hogmanay, the Gifting of Another Year

The end of 2005 has come.
It wears a hat like a scar.
I am alone in a house fretted with
silence. I am the silence.
Music fills some chinks. The house,
an old dog, shakes its coat of paint.
As the year sputters I feel chill.
The calendar is light as ash,
its frangible pages almost wings ...

Corey Mesler

Land of the Lost

Can't put the rain back in the sky
When it falls down, please don't cry.
—Lucinda Williams

Children, the things we lost
we lost because of the spin,
the cranky axis. Let it be.
We are only flesh, children,
only stars fallen and never
returned. Only children, too,
everyone, here on this last wild ride

Our Shortened Days

The recent quake in Chile
may have skewed the entire planet's
axis, shortening our days.
I did not make this up. A NASA
scientist said it today.
And it seems just to me. No flood
this time, just the gradual
reduction of time, just the shaving
off of a few minutes here and there.
I already feel it. I do. So I am
writing as fast as I can. I am reading
as fast as I can. And you, my
family, I pledge to love you exceptionally
hard in these coming days, brief
as dew drops engilt of the provisional sun.

History Tollbooth

Christopher Columbus died as his
slippered foot touched the New Land.
He disintegrated
and his voice became a wave.
Became a dream.
Became sand in a tilted hourglass.

Today I Am Curing Myself

Today I am curing myself
with sugar and a Raymond Chandler
novel. I have sicknesses
that require the absenting from my
life those things which
you and I formerly found instructive.
Today I am giving the Q-tips
a wide berth. Today I am writing on
the board a thousand times:
I am That Which is Not Afraid.
Today I am trying to get in touch
with people who once loved me.
I am not really sick, I will tell them,
not really sick in a way I can explain.
Today I am curing myself
with breadsticks and a Billy Wilder
movie. Today I am thinking about you,
how sick you were, back then, how contagious.

Corey Mesler

Night Like a Thief's Pocket

Light-headed
as if turned on

I stumble back into your arms

pitying the darkness
which used to hold for me

such dense pleasures.

How and Why

A new sheet
as white as
winter's frost unkind.
A word, a mis-
begotten word,
that trips over its own
feat, that lands here
because it is a net.
An idea, the ghost
of a thought
once thought
unimpeachable, a
new idea. And
on and on, into
the spotty part
of the day, the part
where people
start to arrive,
one by one,
with their wit and
their love and
their resolute humanness.

The Middle-of-the-Night Puzzle

It's 2:45 a.m.
and I am already up
for the day.
Nausea woke me,
a foulness inside
that wants out,
like a cur.
I take what drugs I have.
There is small comfort
in Red Rock West
on Showtime. I watch it
in its entirety until
I finally am able to
move around comfortably.
I make coffee for my
sleeping wife and daughter.
It's only 5 a.m. by now.
The day is still a
rebus and I am still a
foul man, wrapped in
his own disorder.

Equilibrium

I must stay on an even keel.
I take a pill to blunt the giddy.
This is why I sleepwalk toward you,
my last best love, my novel.

Aubade

Getting up, moving around,
cleaning yourself, making coffee
—all this is a way of shaking off
 the night's hoodoo and engaging with
 the world.
The first step is the hardest, the cold
floor, the shaky heart.
The kitchen will shine with fairy light.
The globe in the living room
glows like the forehead of morning.
And your book awaits you,
resting on the coffee table where you
placed it when you thought
you would never again fit in. You
reach out your hand and the book
opens to the page where
you became The Reader. The book says,
The day is opening like a melting cluster.
The body is as ready as a church.
And your head is free of webs, free of
sleep virus, and ready for sport.
It is ready for hortatory life, Bright One.

You, Dancing

Stephanie again ...

The San Andreas was
not my fault.
Anything you could read
on a graph was beyond
my ken. I
followed you the way a
moon follows its planet.
You danced
and I watched, a dummy,
a marionette.
When the night ended,
in-
variably I went home alone.
What waited for me
there was
a different kind of rift. I
felt the tremors
of lonesome strata. I felt
you dancing
inside me still, so unstill.

Corey Mesler

Eremite

The wall of my cave is
covered with the bright art
of the children.
The entrance is guarded
by a sheepherding crackie.
The machine that tethers me here
is ancient. In its guts
lie the makings of every book
known to Man.
Sometimes, if the sun intrudes,
it lures me outside a bit.
I stand and crane my neck around,
in perfect imitation of
a man with something on his mind.
Mostly, though, there is just
me and the cave and
the children and the richest poss-
ibilities for accomplishment that
the rusting alphabet can proffer.

In Living Backwards Merlin

In living backwards
Merlin entered lives through
the rear entrance
and bade farewell on the
welcome mat.
He saw the sun roll across the
sky like a bright marble.
He saw the night come on like
a panther dressed for a ball.
I met him once in a dream.
He put his hand on my forehead,
like a stoic father,
and smiled that smile that smells
faintly of doom.
He said, Little man, keep writing.
In the end I have seen
great beginnings. In the end,
a way to start the day without guile.

Corey Mesler

Asleep at the Verso and Recto

In the dark
the words on the page
disappear.
So the power of books
is a limited power.
I lie down uneasy.
Next to me
a Saul Bellow novel
sighs.
Sometime near the
coming of light
I fall quickly
and
without rancor
into a pitifully
dreamless sleep.
A sleep of unheard stories.

Winter AM

The table is bare.
I eat
the cold morning
in silence.
Somewhere in the
nearby
a man like me wakes.
He finds
the ashes in his shoes.
He speaks
my name aloud
though we have never met.
I stare at
the window, grey with
rime. I know
at some point I will go
outside.
He starts a note to me:
I am lonely.
My soul left at sunrise.
I will find you,
my angel, my eudemon.

The Tiniest Child

I found her in the fireplace ashes,
the tiniest child you've ever
seen. I keep her
by me, in a matchbox bed.
Some mornings
she wakes so slowly
my breath stops.
Before sleep she tells
me things only the dead know.
She tells me I am
a giant with an immortal heart.
She tells me I remind her of God.

Wamble Morning

On this pallid morning
I pursue nausea
as it pursued me.
I wash my face in yearn.
The room sweats,
contracts, moves in on me.
The floor is cool
and hard. I put my head
there and feel the
earth below, an ambulance.
On this morning
I feel the nausea quit the
scene like an actor
booed. I am grateful for
the buttery sliver
of light on the throw rug,
thrown too far away.
I wake up again, this
time undreamed.
I lick my wounds. I
take deep breaths of hanker.
I wait for the sanative kiss.

Nihilarian

With the eyes of a child
I saw my work destroyed,
my poems cut apart for
words to make pies.
I stood off to the side and
when I had lost everything
I began to work with my hands.
With them I fashioned
a new self, one not given
to statements, one not given at all.

Effloresce

I have a lot of time
on my hands.
It does not wash away
easily. Like
Lady Macbeth I rub
till I am raw.
You come to me with
an empty basket.
I smile like a pip.
My hands wring time,
over and over,
for its fruits, its flowers.

Corey Mesler

The Invisible Man

I am the invisible man.
It says it on my t-shirt
but my t-shirt is invisible, too.
This is my disclaimer: I will
try to keep my appointments
but I might not show.
I delay, I dither till all the
lights are green. All the
lights are never green. I can
only do one waiting room at a time.
I will be the one with the
bandages over my face. My face
that is invisible. My face
that I show to the children so they
will not be afraid. See, it is nothing.
I am the invisible man.
Look upon me and understand: I
am marginalized, the smudge
at the very edge of your sight, the
man who always wishes
that he could be there.

The Marriage in the Middle of the Night

At 2 a.m.
I pass my wife coming
out of the bathroom.
She has a small bladder.
My wakefulness
is something more baneful,
 a misalignment
of the soul perhaps.
The dawn is distant,
a smudge of light
that will allow me to walk
around as if I belong.
Still, for a few hours after
sunrise I will be
tethered to 2 a.m. and its
dark necromancy.
My wife and I don't talk
about it. The middle
of the night is our crucible.
The middle of the
night is our conformation.

Corey Mesler

Why I Am a Painter

for Rebecca, for Debra

I bought some paint and some canvas
because I tired of the poem,
its grubby little voice, its essence
as feeble as a ghost's.
I wanted something my fingertips
could trace, something as
burly as the pain of waking every
morning. I thought paint
would be that succedaneum. I thought it
could replace every vapory
poem, crowd them all into silence and
muscle them back into the
dark from whence they came. I took
the brush and studied its tip.
I looked at my box of colors.
It seemed worlds of possibility opened
for me, worlds as solid as
the pillar of the Cyclops.
I called my first painting "Poem." I
called my second "Poem II."
I painted and painted until I became
near mute, until I became the quiet man at last,
the man I told myself I wanted to be,
a man who whispers because he is irrefutable.

Mortmain

The often stifling influence of the past.
The way you stood at the door,
your shadow a tear in time/space.
If I remember brown I remember you.
The way your hair fell over your eye.
The time you took me into the bath.
How you touched me. How you touched me.
The often stifling influence of the past.
How when it goes it doesn't stay gone.
How when it's gone it continues to go.
The sleep I've lost. The time I've spent.
If I remember black I remember your eyes.
The way the bed shook with our thrashing.
The way the thrashing led to nothing.
The way feeling died along the way.
The often stifling influence of the goddamn past.

Corey Mesler

Plastic Sun

Earth at the best/Is but a scanty toy—
—Emily Dickinson

Emily also says, we must reverse
the zodiac. I pay
attention, beginning at the beginning,
the one God did in the dark.
This little marble, spinning so consistently
we barely feel it, is
as hospitable as a breathing shell.
It is where I have come to rest. My rest is
occasionally disturbed by a
new planet moving in, a round little poem,
circling the plastic sun.

The Hawk and Mouse in My Backyard

Standing at my kitchen window
I watched a hawk
first play with a helpless mouse
then carry it away.
In the city this is as close as we
get to the untamed, to the
natural. We understand death,
though. We understand
helplessness. Later that night I
went to bed early,
with the new Lorrie Moore novel,
and was asleep by nine-thirty.
In my dreams there were wide open
fields, savannahs and wild profusion
as far as the eye could see. And in
the dream the eye could
see forever. The eye could see it all.

Corey Mesler

Some Concrete Thoughts About the Middle of the Night

The soul is a knitted cap, worn
at the edges. The
eye is futzed like a dirty windscreen.
The gut is too alive, a
monster in the basement lab, joining
the living with a horrific roar,
hungry for the neighborhood children.
The head is stone.
And somewhere in the maelstrom is the
I that writes, squeaking like a door,
I I I, into the cinereal vacuum.

One Afternoon

Patty came home and her
mother was gone. Her
dog had eaten her dinner.

A note taped to the TV
read: Your hamster's dead.
Don't touch the paregoric.

Daddy's bowtie wiggled down
the hall toward her. All the
beds were full of melons.

In the bathroom the faucet played
Ravel. The toilet was full
of tadpoles. Patty sat down
and started her first period.

About the Nothing

She said, Before the
beginning, nothing.
After the last part, nothing.
And in the middle—nothing,
with bright colors.
I said, sit here beside me
and take my hand.
We can watch the wind
change direction. We
can breathe in and out, in and
out. We can see, from here,
where the sky ends like an ellipses.

Meal

The table is set.
It's either dinner or
the devil's game of chance.
The candles are lit
as if by magic.
She smiles at you, a
grimalkin smile.
You hold the food on the
end of your fork.
It's dark as pitch.
It hangs there like a question.
Outside you can hear
the unfurling of wings.
Outside the sun explodes one
last time and falls
into your crystal finger bowl.

Fever

On the couch
I lay
and watched

the suncats
chase a

string of yarn
from
my unknit sleep.

For My Wife of Twenty Years

You were gone for the day visiting your elderly aunt,
discussing difficult things, health, money, end of life.
The house was so still. A peace pervaded. There
was peace in our haphazard arrangement
of things, the objects on surfaces, the spines of books
shelved in descending size, the soft layer of dust as if a peri
had passed. Last night I watched a Rossellini film alone in
my room. You and Chloe were in the front room
doing something with yarn, a woman's art, beyond my
simple understanding. I went to sleep early after a difficult
day, a day of stomach ills and dark thoughts. Yet,
this morning I woke free of those things. My wings
 had returned. I am writing this now, alone in the stillness,
thinking of the gift you are, the way you are, the way you exist.
 I make this simple poem for you. It too is made of stillness
and the desire to know why things come and go, things like peace
and reason. Yet we remain, strong as the enginery that works the
world.

Corey Mesler

How I Changed With the Story

I wrote a story so short
some of the characters
never showed up.
I sent it to my favorite
magazines, the ones
with snow on the covers,
the ones that read the
Slovak writers.
They all added their own
words, each to each,
returning it,
until the story was
swollen like a river.
Swollen like a bruise.
I looked at the new story
and decided to
become someone else,
someone capable
of writing this longer story.
It is now under con-
sideration with all the Big
Boys. I have high hopes for it
and for myself, living
now in a new city
with a new name and a fresh
perspective on my own limitations.

The Two-Prostitute Race

The two-prostitute race
began. We failed to
pick a favorite.
The two-prostitute race
was held under a sun
so hot we thought it was new.
By nighttime it was the
same old sun, set in its
ways, gone. The darkness
moved in, cold, bony,
relentlessly loving and cruel.

Corey Mesler

David Markson Is Dead

From future transmigrations save my soul.

—DM

David Markson is dead.
The place where he stood
is paved with snow.
There is an undimmed spot in
my head where his novels
opened me. Today I am sad
and tonight I will be sad.
Under the reading lamp is a
black pool. I will not read.
My mouth is full of old wind.
David Markson is dead
and his books are moving a-
round in me like fretful memory.

Vertigo

Hitchcock
had it right:
the fall
from a stepstool
is equal to
the fall
from a ledge.
Is equal to
falling in love,
with an eidolon,
with a ghost.
The planet tilts,
one only wants
rootedness,
only wants
the spinning to
stop, or turn
into, if not a thrill,
at least an
acceptable
reaction to the
jeopardous world,
the one far below,
the one
of the madcap heart.

Corey Mesler

Further Conversations With My Dog

When I return from working
at the Synod
my dog greets me at the door.
She says
that dinner will be a little late
tonight. I pat
her head anyway. She's reading
the new Pynchon
and I am working my way through
The Poky Little Puppy.
After we eat—a selection of foreign
cheeses, blood sausage,
eggs—we talk
about the television. I insist that
sports is still a valid
salvation. She says that Animal
Planet has too many commercials, too
few talking dogs.
Before we go to bed with our books
we pray aloud. She says,
Father, let me understand the ways of
Man. I ask simply for
the health of my dog. She is
really the living end. I give her the
last word and she says,
our heartsease is busy being born.

Outside Again

I stood outside.
My chains were made of ice.
I spoke your name
to the snowman's body.
Around us the air crackled
and split, the trees shook
like a debauched swan.
I could not move.
I spoke your name to the sun
as it wound down, to
the ground as it swelled, to
the sky and the sky answered.
It said, you don't deserve your
chains. They shine like diamonds!

The Brief Respite

It was a brief respite.
God took His thumb off
our napes. Some of
us began to speak of going
outside again. Those
who had huddled over pots
of ice, those who were
entomorphagous or ate
matzo for weeks. It was a
brief respite. The rain held
off, then came in cataracts.
We could not see what was
in front of us and we had
forgotten everything else.
We only wanted what any
people want, a time to
gather together to see what
we all thought, a place to
feel like we were viable.
God stepped back to survey
us *in toto*. We looked like
a new experiment, a culture
divided, dividing, finally
able to give ourselves a name,
a prayer we would never forget,
a name that sounded like *vulgus*.

Show Some History

The roadhouses were all dark.
The travelers, left
to their own devices, chose accident
as their default function.
The moon, never that trustworthy
to begin with, disappeared.
The woman with me reached out
and touched me like an abyss.
She said, come over here and take
a piece of me. I told her,
show some history. I am weakened
by the emotions I never
used. I am drifting, drifting, a man
made of fluttering, vanishing skills.

Stranded in the Hebetudes

How to fight today's
hebetude, how to
wrangle when strangled
by the heavy coat?
How to say to you,
so far away you might be
a star, that I write only
to get something back?
How to set them up
to shoot them down
when there is a line at the
fresh muse? I ask these
things because you
are so far away, because
if you knew what was
behind the curtain you
would never answer me.
You would never answer
me. You would say that
I was someone who
loved you once, that old
lie, and that now I am
only a string of similes.
How to fight you when
you have all the right words?
How to even, even, even,
start the stiff sentence?

My Dishy Canadian Cousin

for Debra

When we were younger,
and she was younger, too,
she could make the lights come on.
If we tried to talk to her
it came out jabberwocky; we were
monkeys. She was the daughter
of our most beautiful aunt.
She had her mother's grace, her
mother's perfect cheekbones,
eyes that came from some other place.
Now we are adults with children
older than we were then.
Now we write to each other and there
is still a *frisson*, as if in the
cold hearth an ember suddenly sparked.
When we were younger,
and she was younger, too,
we thought she was
as lovely as the first green in the wood.
Today, I think so, too, though now I
can talk to her. Time heals
some foolishnesses. I say to her,
you made us sweat. You
turned us into jackasses as surely as
smoking would have.
And I say to her, you are still lovely,
like your own paintings, like
the maiden moon, the one that
lights my sleepless nights, my late life.

Corey Mesler

Pother

The dust devils
gather as if on a playground.
The stove looks
like a Pollock dropcloth.
I raise my hand
to signal it's time for me
to go out. My head,
a place of wild bewilderment,
wobbles on its stalk.
All old friends gone now
wait by the pool
to catch my final reflection.
I tell them tales from
the dark inside my head.
I tell them I still love them
like the ticking of a death watch.

Zeus Couldn't Keep It in His Pants

He didn't have a flaw
like Achilles.
He really was a forbidding presence.
But, as a friend of mine
once told me,
he thought with his dick.
It all transpired anyway, the full
story, the one we still tell,
about the brood of gods, and the
whole cataclysmic empty-the-world war.

House Boat

The house was as still
as a docked ship.
Some nights I have to
take it out on the sea
just to feel it shift beneath
me the way the earth
feels on those mornings
I wake with the fear.

86

Halfway Through

The way to the child is blocked
with pain. The path,
once shining, now meanders
through sties and deep
woods. In the morning the face
in the mirror is cockeyed,
the mouth half a frown. Age is
a rusty spoon. I step out
into the sunshine as if it were
a refreshing shower. The
trees mock me with their black
etchings. The shadows mock
me with their secret shapes.
I am all alone again: halfway
through is not good enough anymore.

Jesus Was a Proper Noun

Jesus was a Proper Noun.
He and his twelve participles
dined al fresco,
breaking bread like diagramed
sentences. His sentence
was the ultimate parsing
and his time on the cross,
dangling like a conversation, with
no last minute call
from the governor, a
solecism that has lived
down through the ages like the
myth regarding endings
with a preposition. Jesus died,
saying, Study me. Build
the New Jerusalem from
fresh words, a holy new grammar.
My end is not a period, but an ellipses ...

In Winter, Outside

I lay outside in the leaf-rot
asking only that nature
take me like a naked child.
The night grew cold
and my bones as brittle as
faith. I breathed in
and out, enough motion to
awaken in me things that
I normally assume are missing.

The Writing of the Poem

What leads you away is not what
will lead you back.
The trail of bread crumbs becomes
a path of light. The
words which were formerly so com-
fortable now clang.
What leads you away is not what
will lead you back.
Sometimes it's just a way to teach
the darkness new tricks.

Light to Light

Through nausea,
through life-fear,
through palsy,
I travel like light.
At the end of the
tunnel another light
waits. Its purpose
is to add metaphor
to damaged meat.
Its purpose is not
as plain as the sur-
rounding darkness,
which may stand for
fear, or debility.
Still, I travel. Still I
travel, a loose thread.

Corey Mesler

John Updike Is Gone

John Updike is gone now,
there is little to do about it.
He filled shelves with his
output, Herculean, with that
kind of muscularity, too.
Now I pick a book at random,
a slim early novel, and its
austerity appeals to me, here in
the opening chapter of Spring,
in Memphis where books
are not as honored as one would
wish. I put my nose to its
gutter. John Updike is still gone.
I go back to what I was reading
before this woe interrupted
me: Walter Kirn's *The Unbinding*.

Curandero

It's dark in here with the drugs.
I take all morning
to find the calm. By dinner the
things you brought me
were withering like fruit. I put
my head out the window
to feel the sleet. At night before
sleep I can
hear all the drugs moving around.

Some of the Dharma

The lion under the bed
is mine. I've used it
a thousand times.
I've woken up to nothing
before; I've woken
up to you. The mantra
I've been using is this: ___   .
The letters in my box
are mostly from
the alphabet. The other
half is more sensible.
Or sensitive. The flower
I pull is tough like
a pug. The last word is
stronger than the deluge strong.
I've learned. I'm
applying only some of it.

She Wore the Wound

She wore the wound
the way you or I
might wear a stone.
The stone is worn
by eons of instable
weather. The weather
affects her wound.
On cold nights she stays
home and cries softly
into it, as if it were
a hole one might sud-
denly find in one's side.

In Jackson, Mississippi

I remember you bent over the antique bed
in your house in Jackson, Mississippi.
The bed was white as the inside of an apple.
Your body was an arc of pleasure.
When I entered you it was like
entering rain. You reached around and
held me in place, a touch not unlike love.
I said, you are such a wonderful lover,
and you returned the lob. Days went
by and weeks and months. I divorced a
terrible wife. You found another man to lie
in that bed and watch you ride him
as if he were as solid as a root. I wept be-
cause I was surrounded by loss. I wept
because you were as sexy as a blaze
and I knew, oh, that as much as
twenty years later I would write this poem.

1728 Dashes Equal a Gallon

If we were a measuring people
and, at times, we are,
we would say it's still a long
time between victories.
Except the small ones, of
course, the ones secretaries and
pet owners notate.
If we were a measuring people
we might say that today
we're coming up a little short.
We might say, I loved you
when things were golden, when
our arms browned in the sun.
We might say, between
you and me, there is a gulf as large
as the poles asunder.
We might say, let's count up all
those moments, slipping
through our hands like sands,
until we are beached.
We might say, come closer,
just for tonight, with the light the
way it is, having come so
far to empurple our gloaming,
light years uncountable, if
we were, if we were a measuring people.

Corey Mesler

Evenfall

At dusk I took my pad
onto the porch and
tried to wrestle the crimson
sky into six lines. I
give up now. I have lost faith
in the opaque, charcoal line.

Seizure

The sickness of angels is nothing new.
I have seen them crawling like bees ...

—Mark Strand

When Chloe seized
my eyes went black.
I saw nothing.
I saw too much.
I was a nerve, scraped.
Fear wanted
another word for fear.
Now it's years ago.
And these are the
first words enlisted,
because vocabulary
is a weak tincture,
because vulnerability
is still there, like a tear,
like an abyss. On
that morning I prayed
as if I had never
prayed before, the ur-
prayer, the commencement.
When Chloe seized
I went wordless, I
went blind, I went forth to
petition the humid heavens,
with silence, eyeless.

Brumal Song

The day is the color of no-color.
Our home, where we have
come to believe,
has walls like mesh. Such is
our cage made, such
is our cave. Today it's in the
teens and there are
comforters and afghans piled on
the couch. We sit there,
using them like sand bags,
to watch the war on television.
In this snow it is
hard to see who is winning. Most
nights we think we are.

Starring Erica Rhodes

I wrote a new poem.
It stars that ingénue,
Erica Rhodes.
She appears in line seventeen,
kicks things around,
and is gone by the end
of the third verse. Her beauty
threatens to throw the
whole poem off balance. Her
face the face the sky would
wear if the sky were to
wear a face. The poem limps
toward an inconclusive
conclusion. Its star is gone.
The rest of the cast
do their best. The poem re-
fuses to come alive like
Persona or anything by
Frank O'Hara or
Jacques Tati.
The poem loves Jacques Tati.
Its real death occurs near
the penultimate line.
Over its spooled shoulder,
the poem looks back at
Erica Rhodes,
a wanton, stilted enthrallment,
wanting to try again with her,
as its credits roll like a
frolic of architecture.

Corey Mesler

The Voice and Me

The Voice that Wants my Annihilation waits in line at the Jiffy Stop. I feign interest in the Hostess rack to avoid His eye. I hear Him ask, too loudly, for a lottery ticket. "Do not scratch here," the young Korean man says. The Voice looks around to see if anyone is witness. His gaze rakes over me like a small tool grooming its bonsai bed. It's too hot in the Jiffy Stop because outside it is too cold. After The Voice leaves I feel as if I should purchase something. I get some chemical cakes and the latest issue of Boobs. The young Korean man rings up my sale and smiles at me. "You writer," he says. I shake my head. What if The Voice that Wants my Annihilation were somehow still listening? I do not want Him to know of my ability to limn him in print, to mask my fear of him behind irony, lucubration, feminine rhyme or syzygy. As if He is an ex-wife I want Him to think I still love Him. I go home and study the small pastry I have bought to see if there is something there about which to write a tanka. The phone rings. I know it is The Voice calling. I want so badly to finish something before I answer His call. I want so bad to finish one small thing before I answer His call.

Poem for Amanda After Reading Hers

*How do you have those kinds of thoughts a poet has where a
stone becomes a song ...*

—Amanda Bausch

I have known stones that sing.
Jesus is my goad.
I have known songs that last so
long they break the air
into disjecta membra.
I have sung and in singing for-
gotten the promises
I made to my godling.
In the sunlight these songs know
the shadows poems know.
Amanda, I can only use words
as the roughest of tools, to
hone the stone toward singing. I
can only count the songs
that have died from lack of the
very thing I thought I
had cleared from my claptrap life.

Corey Mesler

Others

My lovely neighbor must be sleeping naked,
Or lighting a match to see what time it is.
—Charles Simic

They're everywhere, other
people. I hear them
moving about
while I am trying to sleep.
I see them
in lines to which I am not
welcome. I listen
to them telling each other
shameful things. I love them
with this fierce and tardy heart,
my better heft, my ache.

Black River

Through my backyard
flows a river, black like love.
Its banks are heaped
with ice; its mouth speaks to
me in the tongue of mansnakes.
I call this river Canticle.
It lets me sleep sometimes
in its flow. It lets me fish
in it for fortune, for moonlight.

I Lay My Head Upon a Stanza

I dreamed a poem.
When I awoke
I found the poem was
my pillow
and my weighty head
had mis-shaped it
until the poem was of
no use. I tried to write
a waking poem,
a poem of engagement,
but I grew quickly bored,
quickly enervated,
and as sleepy as a newborn.

My Son Is Getting Married Today

for Toby, June 15, 2013

My son is getting married
today. The boy
who once left a note
saying: *kis me in*
the morning, be a surpriz.
Today, under the same
sky Adam, holding his
damaged side,
hid from beneath a tree of
knowledge, Toby will
stand and say the
right things. Then he will
board a boat as
large as all of life; he may
turn back once, and wave
for the benefit of all who
stand behind him and
beside him, heart held open.

Path

for Chloe

This is the fairy tale,
the one with
the path, the one with
the darkness.
Take my hand. You
are still wee to me.
Tell me again how you
will grow and love
and prosper. That's the
way I listen. I
listen with my pen. I
listen like starlight,
till the fairy tale
opens its bloody rose.

For Cheryl on Her 46th Birthday

You age and I age
and the house
goes soft. The rooms
get smaller
even as we get smaller.
We love here.
We are the true in-
habitants, the dreamers.

Every Dark (1/1/11)

I write this in the dark.
It's the start of another year
and I am alone and as
blue as a trance.
I write this in the dark
because I am afraid of the
well-lit corners of myself.
I write this in the dark
hoping not to wake you, you
who have stood by me,
in every poem, every dark.

Corey Mesler has published in numerous journals and anthologies. He has published five novels, *Talk: A Novel in Dialogue* (2002), *We Are Billion-Year-Old Carbon* (2006), *The Ballad of the Two Tom Mores* (2010), *Following Richard Brautigan* and (2010), *Gardner Remembers* (2011), 2 full-length poetry collections, *Some Identity Problems* (2008) and *Before the Great Troubling* (2011), and 3 books of short stories, *Listen: 29 Short Conversations* (2009), *Notes toward the Story and Other Stories* (2011) and *I'll Give You Something to Cry About* (2011). He has also published a dozen chapbooks of both poetry and prose. He has been nominated for the Pushcart Prize numerous times, and 2 of his poems have been chosen for Garrison Keillor's Writer's Almanac. With his wife, he runs Burke's Book Store in Memphis TN, one of the country's oldest (1875) and best independent bookstores. He can be found at www.coreymesler.com.

Publication Credits

Grateful acknowledgment to the publications where these poems first appeared:

Adroit
I Didn't Know I Was Going to Do That
Brumal Song

Anomalous Press
1728 Dashes Equal a Gallon

Architrave Press
Seizure

Ardent
Asleep at the Verso and Recto

Big Toe Review
Departure

Bloody Bridge Review
My Heart a Map
You, Dancing

Blue and Yellow Dog
Poem for Amanda After Reading One of Hers
Black River

Bolts of Silk
Fever

Cezanne's Carrot
Hogmanay, the Gifting of Another Year

Corium
Witch Philosophy
Chloe Blooming

DeComp
Aubade

Diverse Voices Quarterly
A White Pause

Drown in My Own Fears
Our Shortened Days
Show Some History

Esopian
It Was Summer, of That I Am Sure

Foliate Oak
I Lay My Head Upon a Stanza

H_NGM_N
Some of the Dharma

Kill Author
Curandero

Leaf Garden
Church
Book
More About Wendy Ward
In This Atmosphere
In Jackson, Mississippi
I Didn't Know It Was Going to Be a Frank O'Hara Day

Our Locust Years

The Legendary
Iconolatry
Again Lita

Literary Tonic
Mortmain

Mannequin Envy
Shift
Halfway Through

Metazen
Today I Am Curing Myself

Monkey Puzzle
My Dishy Canadian Cousin

Octaves
Land of the Lost

Pank
The Earth Knows My Secret Name
And Her Name Was I Am Not Staying

Poetry Super Highway
The Best Effects Available

Prick of the Spindle
The Brief Respite

Prose Toad
He Sit Ate
We At Her

Psychic Meatloaf
Night Like a Thief's Pocket

Rhino
History Tollbooth

Salt River Review
The Voice and Me

Slingshot
She Wore the Wound
Every Dark
In Winter, Outside

Sparkbright
Winter AM

Steel Toe Review
Path

Tinfoil Dresses
The Two-Prostitute Race
David Markson Is Dead

Tipton Poetry Journal
Anticipation Is a Blind Dog in a Meat Shop
Over, Easy

trnsfr
Our Locust Years

Used Furniture Review
The Tiniest Child

Our Locust Years

Vehicle
Others

Verse Wisconsin
Why I Am a Painter

Viral Cat
Eremite
In Living Backwards, Merlin

wft pwm
Vertigo

XConnect
Writing Myself

ΥB
Out Near the Chemical Plant

Praise for *Our Locust Years:*

Corey Mesler is a poet of intimacy and honesty with a gift for memorable lines and phrases such as "a chapel shaped like a farm," and "She entered my life / like a battered dresser, all / drawers open ... " His poems are intimate, wistful, and often erotic. Though he does not go out of his way to establish settings and a sense of location, his poems are subtly and yet unmistakably evocative of the city where he lives, particularly of midtown Memphis. Everyone who owns a book or two by Peter Taylor, who loves the music of Booker T and MGs and Jessie Winchester, will want to have Corey Mesler on their bookshelves.

> —Richard Tillinghast, author of *Today in the Cafe Trieste* and
> *The Stonecutter's Hand*

All of us who write hope to be owned by a self beyond the self, in an attitude of what Miss Welty calls honesty, a direct and contemplative relation to time-beings, transformed to figures and sentences. Besides which, as Miss Emily writes, the long haul, toward something we used to call eternity, resides in the moment, not in the clock or calendar. (I put it in the present tense because it does not go away.) Not also but especially in the briefest, the tenderest of moments, when one is possessed by intimacy with his own life, there is no more crowding an enemy than human time. The radicality (I know, there's no such word) of Corey Mesler's poetry is its presentation of the terrific values in pieces of being, in protracted moments of verbal attention, in images that make even the awful and perilous things we know—enlightening.

> —Gordon Osing, author of *Things that Never Happened*

In compellingly direct language, *Our Locust Years* captures a later-life perspective on anxiety, nostalgia, and regret. "Eight years ago / my father left // turning out the light / behind me, // leaving me to bake / a pie / with the scarecrow's bones," reads the entirety of

Departure. Yet there is clever wordplay here, too, as a later poem declares "The San Andreas was / not my fault," and another confesses "I am the invisible man ... I will / try to keep my appointments / but I might not show." With humor and heart, Corey Mesler writes poems of the most sacred purpose—to navigate a better understanding of this complicated, compromised, but ultimately precious world.

—Sandra Beasley, author of *I Was the Jukebox*

Selected Titles Published by Unbound Content

www.ingramcontent.com/pod-product-compliance
Lightning Source LLC
Chambersburg PA
CBHW051732090426
42738CB00010B/2224